Garden Path

Color the boxes from **75** to **100**, in order, to make a path from Start to Finish.

Start

75	76	77	80	81	93	94
78	71	78	79	91	80	83
72	89	79	83	93	94	95
82	81	80	88	92	91	96
83	88	79	72	91	98	97
84	76	75	78	90	92	98
85	86	87	88	89	93	99
88	92	94	93	91	87	100

Finish

Sequencing numbers to 100

1

On the Green

Add.

$9 + 9 =$ _____ 18

$9 + 8 =$ _____

$9 + 7 =$ _____

$10+2=$ _____

$4+6=$ _____

$10+8=$ _____

$8+9=$ _____

$7+9=$ _____

$9+6=$ _____

$8+8=$ _____

$7+3=$ _____

$0+7=$ _____

$2+6=$ _____

$8+0=$ _____

$6+3=$ _____

$5+8=$ _____

$6+6=$ _____

$9+2=$ _____

Finding sums to 18

The Pawprint Marks the Spot

7 + ? = 11

7 + 4 = 11

Write the missing number.

6
+ ⬤
14

+ 9
12

8
+ ⬤
13

+ 9
17

+ 8
16

+ 7
7

9
+ ⬤
18

10
+ ⬤
13

3
+ ⬤
11

+ 7
15

5
+ ⬤
15

Finding missing addends

3

Down We Go

Cross out and subtract.

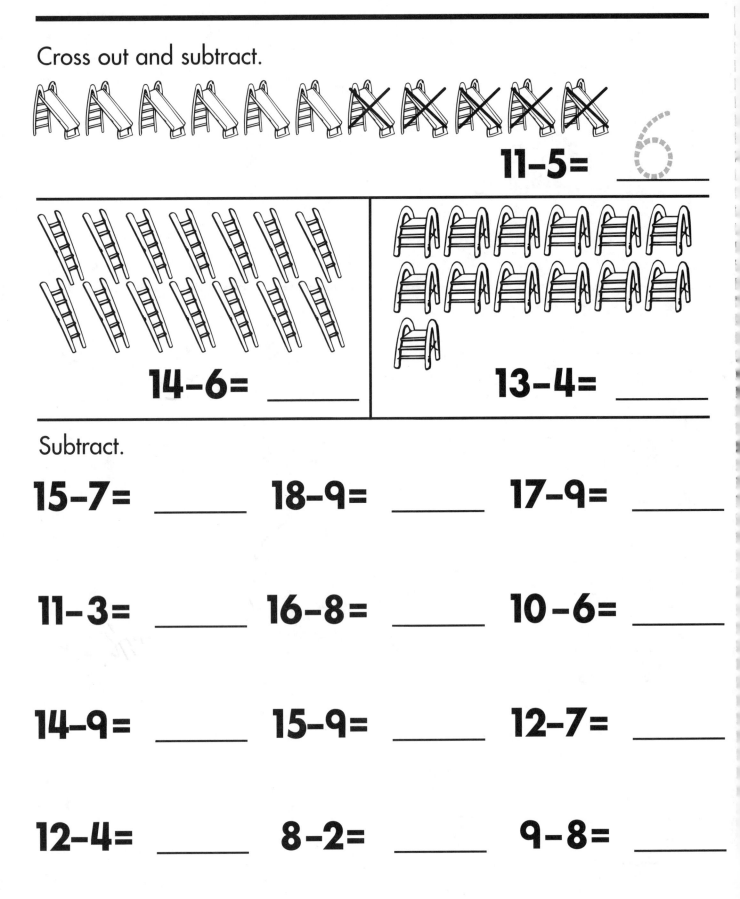

$11-5=$ _____

$14-6=$ _____

$13-4=$ _____

Subtract.

$15-7=$ _____ $18-9=$ _____ $17-9=$ _____

$11-3=$ _____ $16-8=$ _____ $10-6=$ _____

$14-9=$ _____ $15-9=$ _____ $12-7=$ _____

$12-4=$ _____ $8-2=$ _____ $9-8=$ _____

Subtracting from numbers up to 18

Look What's Missing

Write the missing number.

14 − ___ = 6

12 − ___ = 9

___ − 5 = 7

10 − ___ = 7

___ − 8 = 8

18 − ___ = 9

13 − ___ = 6

___ − 4 = 8

17 − ___ = 8

___ − 7 = 4

14 − ___ = 9

9 − ___ = 5

___ − 6 = 3

10 − ___ = 8

Climbing Monkeys

Find the pattern. Write the missing numbers.

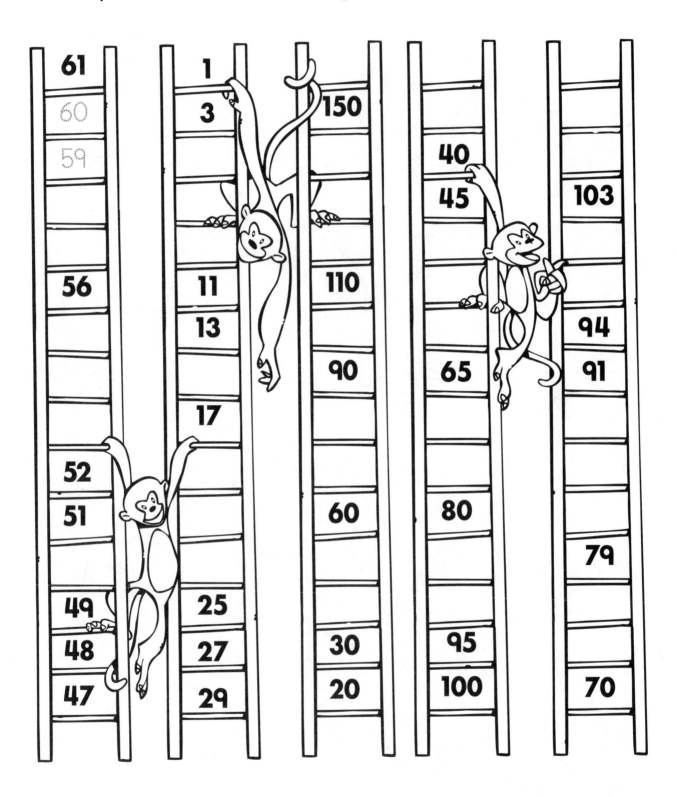

Identifying and continuing number patterns

Pizza Order

45   **54**   **60**

The numbers from **least** to **greatest** are 45, 54, and 60.

Write each group of numbers from **least** to **greatest**.

10	30	20
10	20	30

18	23	14
__	__	__

45	48	52
__	__	__

34	41	29
__	__	__

60	47	59
__	__	__

75	57	68
__	__	__

35	27	31
__	__	__

67	82	53
__	__	__

90	68	77
__	__	__

Number Quackers

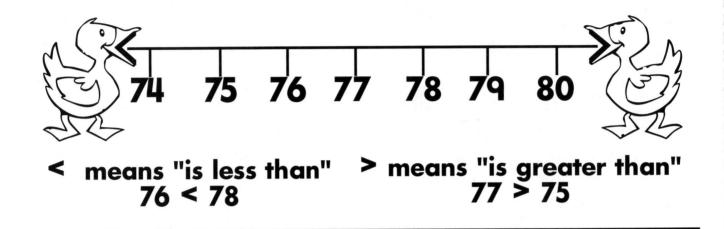

< means "is less than"
76 **<** 78

> means "is greater than"
77 **>** 75

Complete each sentence with **< or >**.
Be sure the duck's mouth is open to the greater number.

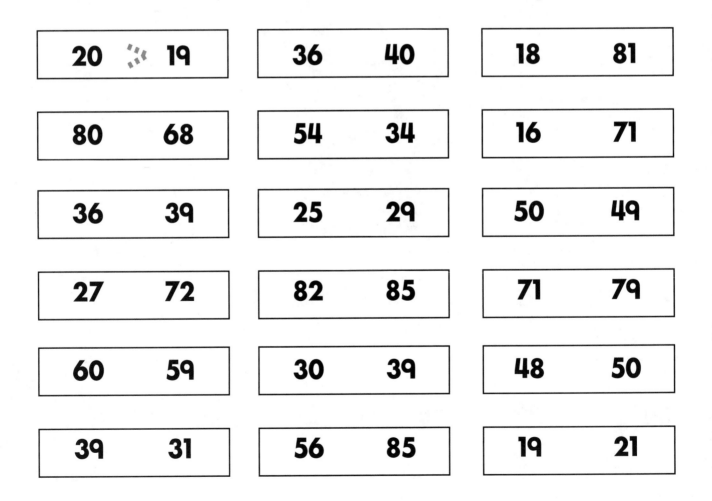

20 ⟩ 19	36 40	18 81
80 68	54 34	16 71
36 39	25 29	50 49
27 72	82 85	71 79
60 59	30 39	48 50
39 31	56 85	19 21

Using inequality signs to compare 2-digit numbers

Match Game

Draw lines to match.

8 tens and 3 ones	97	fifty-eight
5 tens and 8 ones	58	forty-three
3 tens and 1 one	43	ninety-seven
9 tens and 7 ones	26	eighty-nine
8 tens and 9 ones	64	sixty-four
7 tens and 5 ones	83	twenty-six
6 tens and 4 ones	75	thirty-one
2 tens and 6 ones	89	seventeen
1 ten and 7 ones	31	eighty-three
4 tens and 3 ones	17	seventy-five

Treasure Hunt

Odd numbers end in 1, 3, 5, 7, and 9.
Even numbers end in 0, 2, 4, 6, and 8.
Color treasures with **odd** numbers blue.
Color treasure with **even** numbers yellow.

Identifying odd and even numbers

Sum Elephant

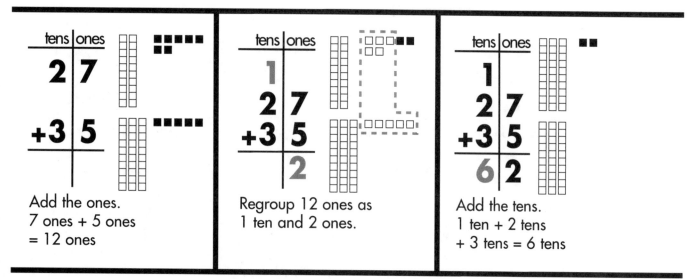

tens | ones

$2 | 7$
$+3 | 5$

Add the ones.
7 ones + 5 ones
= 12 ones

tens | ones

1
$2 | 7$
$+3 | 5$
2

Regroup 12 ones as
1 ten and 2 ones.

tens | ones

1
$2 | 7$
$+3 | 5$
$6 | 2$

Add the tens.
1 ten + 2 tens
+ 3 tens = 6 tens

Write the sum. Circle it if you regrouped.

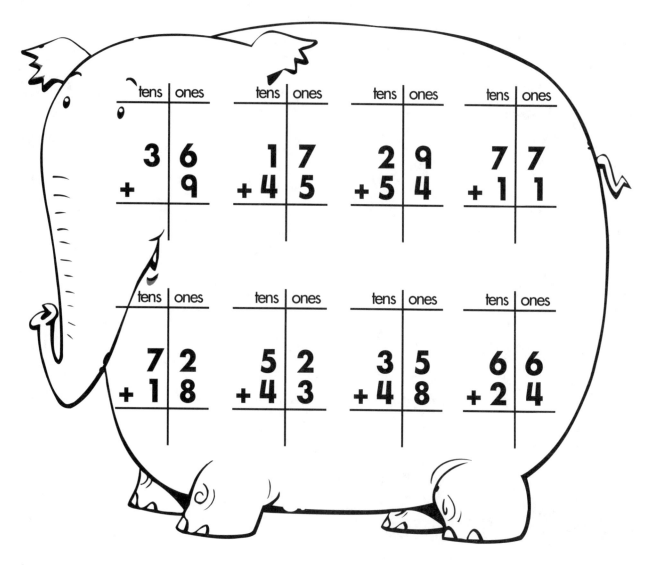

tens	ones
3	6
+	9

tens	ones
1	7
+4	5

tens	ones
2	9
+5	4

tens	ones
7	7
+1	1

tens	ones
7	2
+1	8

tens	ones
5	2
+4	3

tens	ones
3	5
+4	8

tens	ones
6	6
+2	4

Under the Sea

Add. Then use the code to color the picture.

If the sum is between	40-54	55-69	70-84	85-99
Color the creature	Red	Orange	Green	Yellow

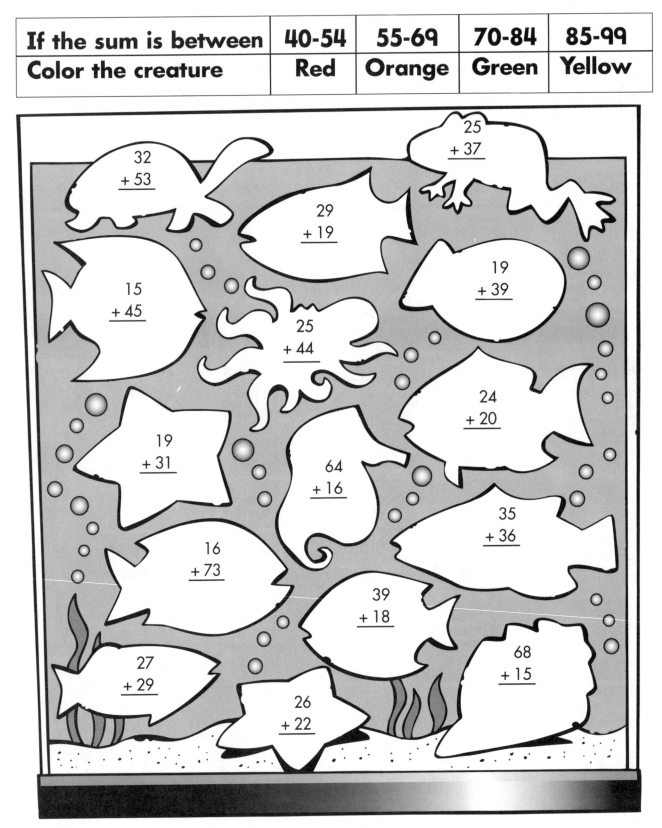

Adding 2-digit numbers with and without regrouping

Hundreds, Tens, and Ones

Write how many hundreds, tens, and ones. Then write the number.

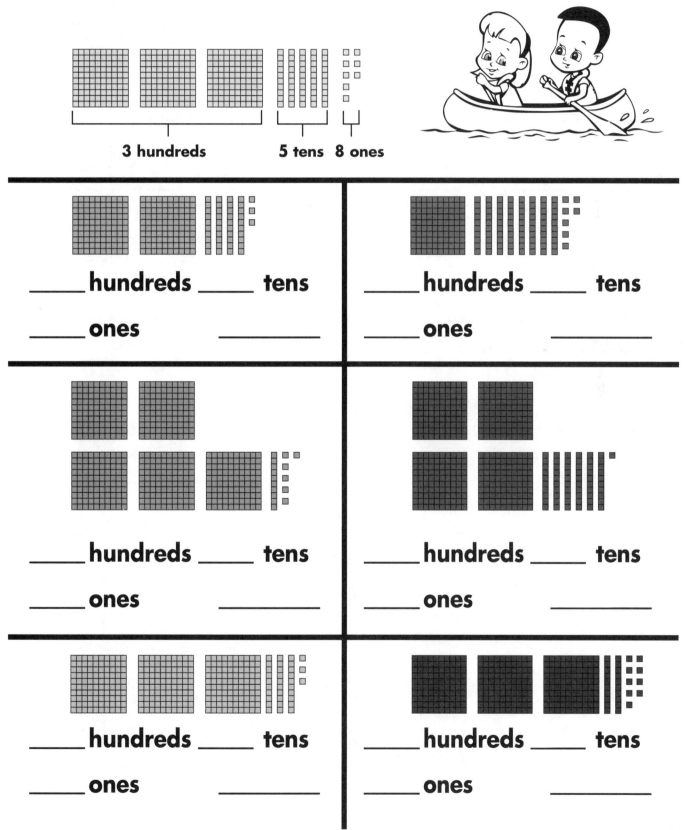

3 hundreds   5 tens   8 ones

_____ hundreds _____ tens

_____ ones   _____

_____ hundreds _____ tens

_____ ones   _____

_____ hundreds _____ tens

_____ ones   _____

_____ hundreds _____ tens

_____ ones   _____

_____ hundreds _____ tens

_____ ones   _____

_____ hundreds _____ tens

_____ ones   _____

Diving for Treasure

hundreds	tens	ones
1	4	7
+5	3	2
		9

Add the ones.
7 ones + 2 ones = 9 ones

hundreds	tens	ones
1	4	7
+5	3	2
	7	9

Add the tens.
4 tens + 3 tens = 7 tens

hundreds	tens	ones
1	4	7
+5	3	2
6	7	9

Add the hundreds.
1 hundred + 5 hundreds =
6 hundreds.
The sum is 679.

First add the ones. Then add the tens. Then add the hundreds.

hundreds	tens	ones
5	1	6
+2	8	0

hundreds	tens	ones
3	4	0
+5	1	8

hundreds	tens	ones
9	4	1
+	2	8

hundreds	tens	ones
3	2	6
+4	5	3

hundreds	tens	ones
4	3	6
+5	3	0

hundreds	tens	ones
8	2	1
+1	6	3

hundreds	tens	ones
	3	4
+8	5	4

hundreds	tens	ones
1	5	2
+7	4	2

hundreds	tens	ones
6	0	7
+2	5	1

Adding 3-digit numbers without regrouping

Ready, Set, Regroup

hundreds	tens	ones
	1	
2	**5**	**8**
+ 3	**9**	**4**
		2

Add the ones.
There are 12 ones.
Regroup 10 ones for
1 ten.

hundreds	tens	ones
1	**1**	
2	**5**	**8**
+ 3	**9**	**4**
	5	**2**

Add the tens.
There are 15 tens.
Regroup 10 tens for
1 hundred.

hundreds	tens	ones
1	**1**	
2	**5**	**8**
+ 3	**9**	**4**
6	**5**	**2**

Add the hundreds.
There are 6
hundreds.
The sum is 652.

Add. Use the example above to help you.

hundreds	tens	ones
4	**3**	**2**
+ 2	**8**	**3**

hundreds	tens	ones
2	**4**	**8**
+ 3	**4**	**6**

hundreds	tens	ones
2	**5**	**6**
+ 3	**3**	**3**

hundreds	tens	ones
3	**6**	**5**
+ 3	**7**	**9**

hundreds	tens	ones
1	**2**	**5**
+	**4**	**9**

hundreds	tens	ones
7	**8**	**4**
+ 1	**6**	**5**

Adding 3-digit numbers with and without regrouping   **15**

Sticker Math

Read each story problem. Write a number sentence and solve.

1. One day, Mr. Perez sells 132 puffy animal stickers and 257 plain animal stickers. How many animal stickers does he sell that day?

_____

2. Mr. Perez orders 527 new shiny stickers and 268 new puffy stickers. How many new stickers does Mr. Perez order?

_____

3. Ms. Ross buys 87 car stickers and 125 happy face stickers. How many stickers does Ms. Ross buy?

_____

4. Julie's scout troop buys 328 puffy stickers and 480 shiny stickers. How many stickers does the troop buy?

5. Mrs. Patel buys 249 "Good Work" stickers and 518 star stickers. How many stickers does Mrs. Patel buy?

6. The Sticker Club buys 375 animal stickers and 297 animal stickers. How many stickers does the club buy?

Solving addition story problems involving 2- and 3-digit numbers

Flying High

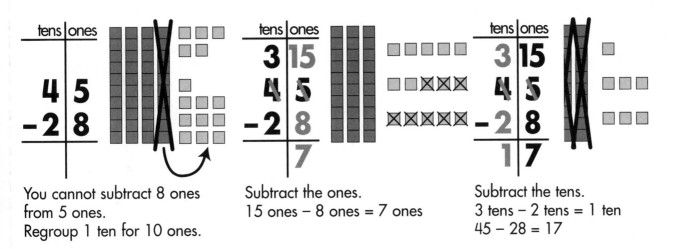

You cannot subtract 8 ones from 5 ones.
Regroup 1 ten for 10 ones.

Subtract the ones.
15 ones − 8 ones = 7 ones

Subtract the tens.
3 tens − 2 tens = 1 ten
45 − 28 = 17

Write the difference. Circle it if you regrouped.

Winning Scores

Circle the greater score.
Then subtract to find out
by how many points the
home team won.

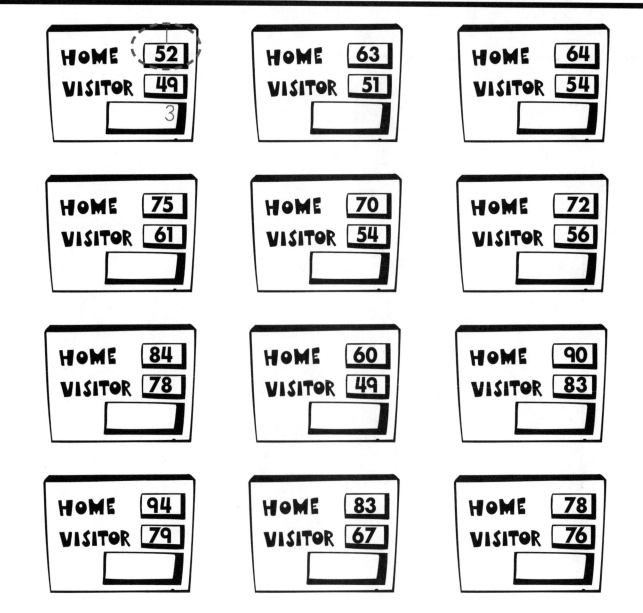

HOME (52)
VISITOR [49]
3

HOME [63]
VISITOR [51]

HOME [64]
VISITOR [54]

HOME [75]
VISITOR [61]

HOME [70]
VISITOR [54]

HOME [72]
VISITOR [56]

HOME [84]
VISITOR [78]

HOME [60]
VISITOR [49]

HOME [90]
VISITOR [83]

HOME [94]
VISITOR [79]

HOME [83]
VISITOR [67]

HOME [78]
VISITOR [76]

Subtracting 2-digit numbers with and without regrouping

Dive Into Subtraction

hundreds	tens	ones
8	4	9
− 5	1	2
		7

Subtract the ones.
9 ones − 2 ones = 7 ones

hundreds	tens	ones
8	4	9
− 5	1	2
	3	7

Subtract the tens.
4 tens − 1 ten = 3 tens

hundreds	tens	ones
8	4	9
− 5	1	2
3	3	7

Subtract the hundreds.
8 hundreds − 5 hundreds =
3 hundreds
The difference is 337.

Subtract.

hundreds	tens	ones
9	7	6
− 3	5	3

hundreds	tens	ones
7	8	5
− 4	8	1

hundreds	tens	ones
5	8	6
− 2	5	4

hundreds	tens	ones
8	3	6
− 5	2	0

hundreds	tens	ones
4	9	8
− 2	5	1

hundreds	tens	ones
3	9	2
−	9	2

All Aboard

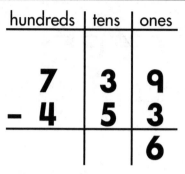

hundreds	tens	ones
7	3	9
− 4	5	3
		6

Subtract the ones.
9 ones − 3 ones = 6 ones

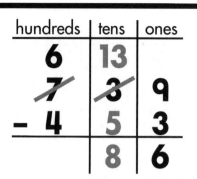

hundreds	tens	ones
6 7̸	1̸3 3̸	9
− 4	5	3
	8	6

You cannot subtract 5 tens
from 3 tens. Regroup
1 hundred for 10 tens.
Subtract the tens.
13 tens − 5 tens = 8 tens

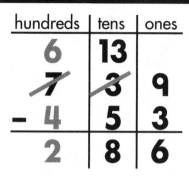

hundreds	tens	ones
6 7̸	1̸3 3̸	9
− 4	5	3
2	8	6

Subtract the hundreds.
6 hundreds − 4 hundreds =
2 hundreds.
The difference is 286.

Subtract. Regroup if you need to.

hundreds	tens	ones
5	3	9
− 1	8	7

hundreds	tens	ones
7	5	2
− 3	4	6

hundreds	tens	ones
6	4	6
− 5	3	3

hundreds	tens	ones
8	6	5
− 3	7	1

hundreds	tens	ones
7	9	7
− 6	4	7

hundreds	tens	ones
6	8	4
− 1	6	5

Subtracting 3-digit numbers with and without regrouping

Take Me Out to the Ball Game

Read each story problem. Write a number sentence and solve.

1. There are 387 boys and 410 girls at the *Stars* game. How many more girls than boys are at the game?

_____

2. There are 797 children and 912 adults at the *Stars* game. How many more adults than children are at the game?

_____

3. Manny sells 425 sodas and 670 bottled waters. How many more bottled waters than sodas are sold?

_____

4. Jane sells 459 bags of peanuts and 953 hot dogs. How many more hot dogs than peanuts are sold?

_____

5. The *Stars* sell 564 pennants. Of those, 181 are small pennants and the rest are large pennants. How many large pennants are sold?

_____

6. The *Stars* give away 175 t-shirts. All but 38 of them are given to children. How many t-shirts are given to children?

_____

7. Mr. Patel has 800 *Stars* baseball caps to sell. He sells all but 282 of them. How many caps does Mr. Patel sell?

_____

8. The *Stars* play 65 games at home out of a total of 123 games. How many games are played away from home?

_____

At the Zoo

Use an inch ruler to measure each path on the map.
Write about how many inches.

How long is the path:

1. From the entrance to the monkey?   _____ inches

2. From the entrance to the snake?   _____ inches

3. From the monkey to the bird?   _____ inches

4. From the snack Bar to the seal?   _____ inches

5. From the elephant to the lion?   _____ inches

6. From the lion to the snake?   _____ inches

    Measuring paths in inches

Find Sam's Sneaker

Use a centimeter ruler to measure the length of each sneaker. Sam's sneaker is 9 centimeters long. Find and color Sam's sneaker.

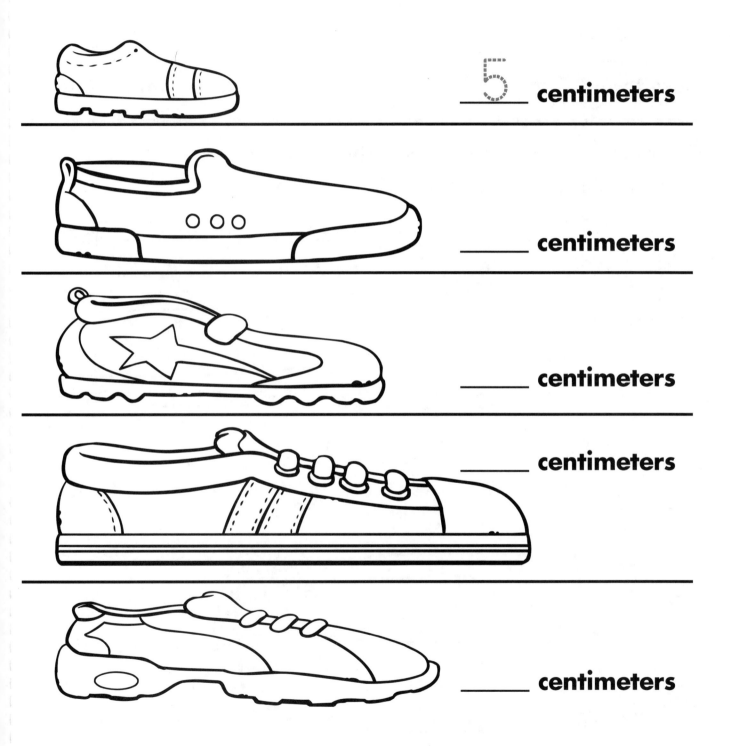

_5__ **centimeters**

_____ **centimeters**

_____ **centimeters**

_____ **centimeters**

_____ **centimeters**

How Much Does It Hold?

less than 1 liter   **1 liter**   **more than 1 liter**

Color the things that hold **more than 1 liter** red.
Color the things that hold **less than 1 liter** yellow.

Comparing the capacity of containers with 1 liter

Cups, Pints, and Quarts

1 cup   **2 cups = 1 pint**   **4 cups = 1 quart**

Color the **cups** to show the same amounts.

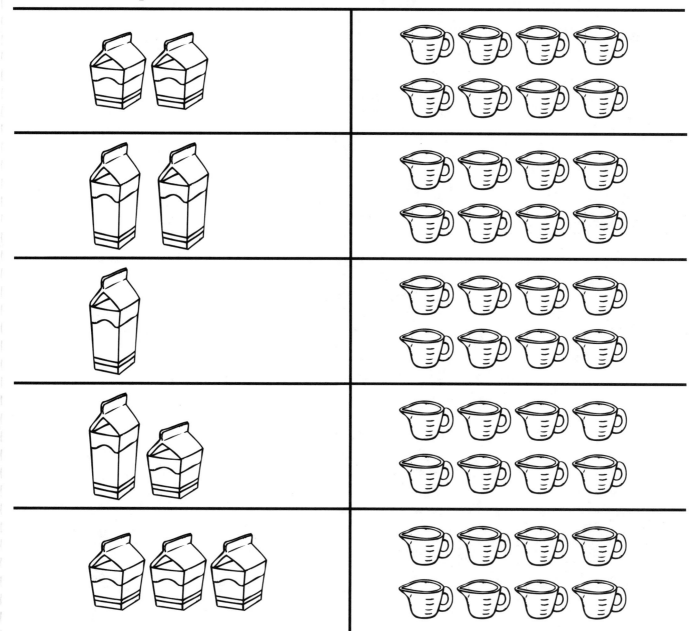

Weighing Pounds

This spaghetti weighs 1 **pound**.
Another way to write **pound** is **lb**.

Color the things that weigh **more than 1 pound** red.
Color the things that weigh **less than 1 pound** blue.

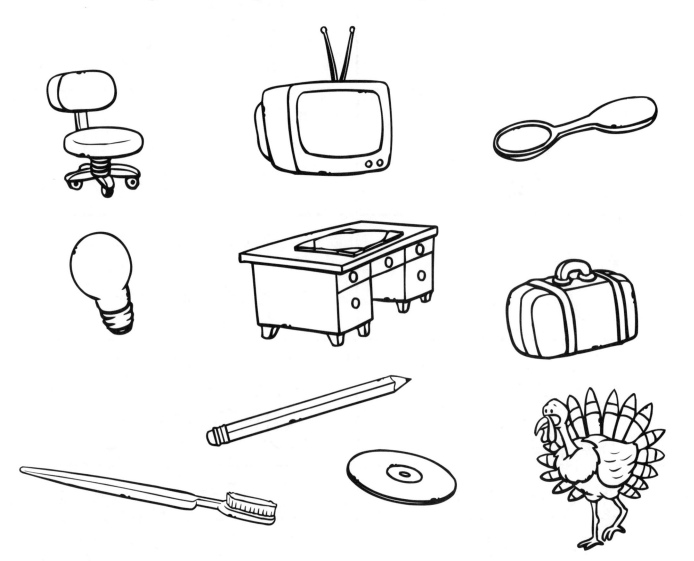

Kilograms

Another way to write **kilogram** is **kg**.

| less than 1 kilogram | about 1 kilogram | more than 1 kilogram |

Color the things that are **more than 1 kilogram** green.
Color the things that are **less than 1 kilogram** orange.

Food for Sharing

Color 1/2 red.

Color 1/3 green.

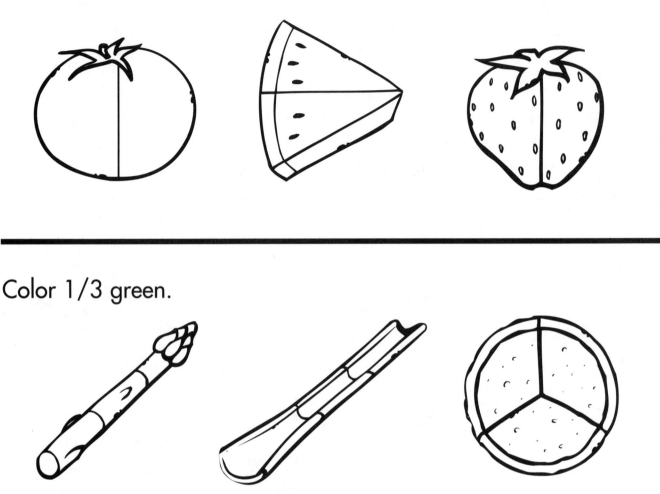

Color 1/4 orange.

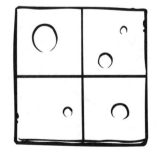

Recognizing halves, thirds, and fourths

Hot or Cold?

Circle the correct temperature.

Write the temperature.

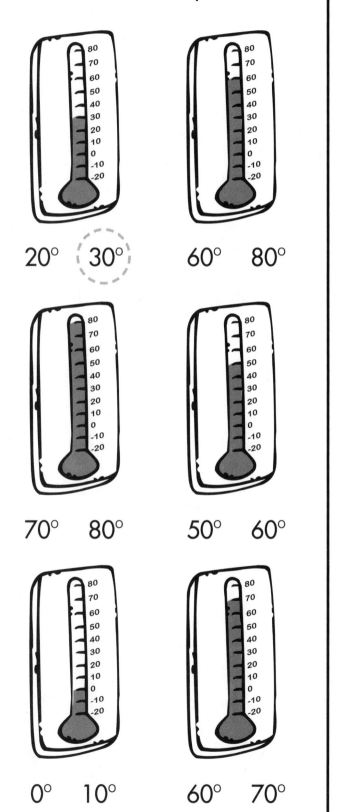

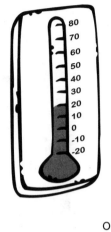

20° (30°)   60° 80°

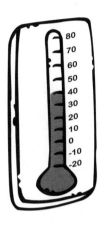

_____ °   _____ °

70° 80°   50° 60°

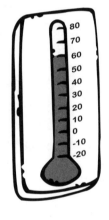

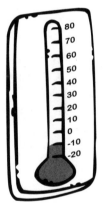

_____ °   _____ °

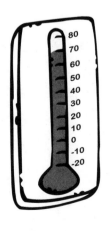

0° 10°   60° 70°

_____ °   _____ °

Happy Birthday

Students were asked when their birthday is. Read the graph to answer the questions.

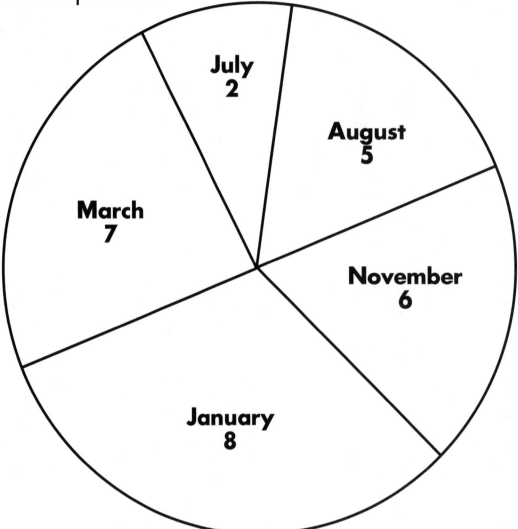

1. How many students were asked when their birthday is? _____

2. How many different months were named? _____

3. How many students were born in August? _____

4. In which month were most of the students born? _____

5. What fraction of students said March? _____

Interpreting a circle graph

Monster Match

Draw lines to match the coins with the amounts on the tags.

Spots, Spots Everywhere

Each bug has the same number of spots. Count or multiply to find how many spots in all.

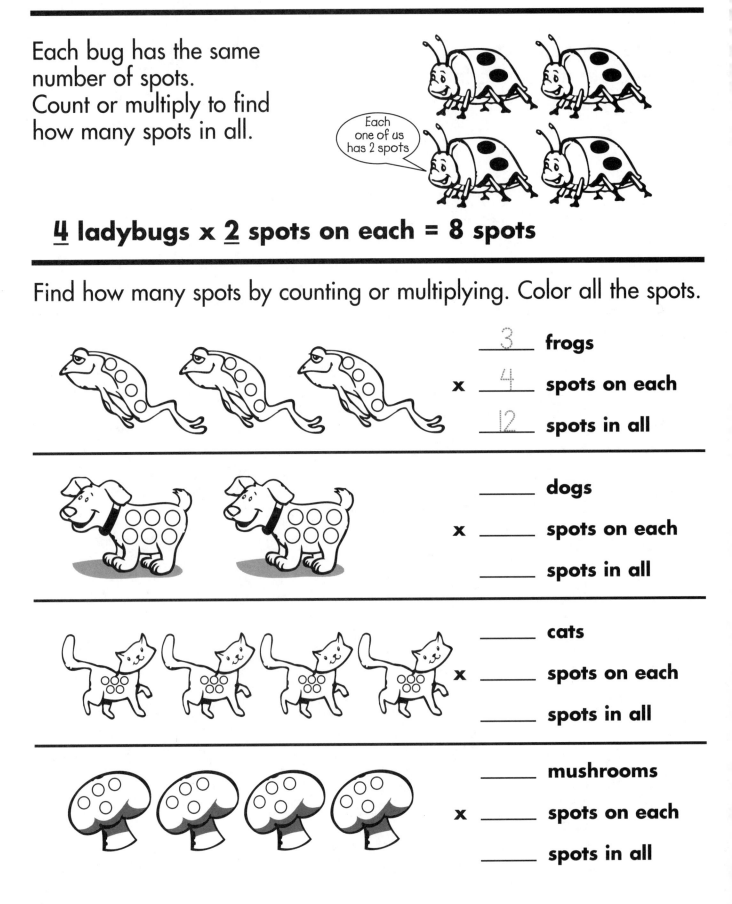

Each one of us has 2 spots

4 ladybugs x **2** spots on each = 8 spots

Find how many spots by counting or multiplying. Color all the spots.

<u>3</u> **frogs**

x <u>4</u> **spots on each**

<u>12</u> **spots in all**

_____ **dogs**

x _____ **spots on each**

_____ **spots in all**

_____ **cats**

x _____ **spots on each**

_____ **spots in all**

_____ **mushrooms**

x _____ **spots on each**

_____ **spots in all**

Combining equal groups

Flower Garden

There are 3 rows of daisies.
There are 5 daisies in each row.
There are 15 daisies in all.

Count how many rows. Count how many in each row.
Write the total.

2 rows of 4 = ___8___

2 x 4 = _____

3 rows of 3 = _____

3 x 3 = _____

3 rows of 4 = _____

3 x 4 = _____

2 rows of 5 = _____

2 x 5 = _____

3 rows of 6 = _____

3 x 6 = _____

4 rows of 5 = _____

4 x 5 = _____

Fruit Times

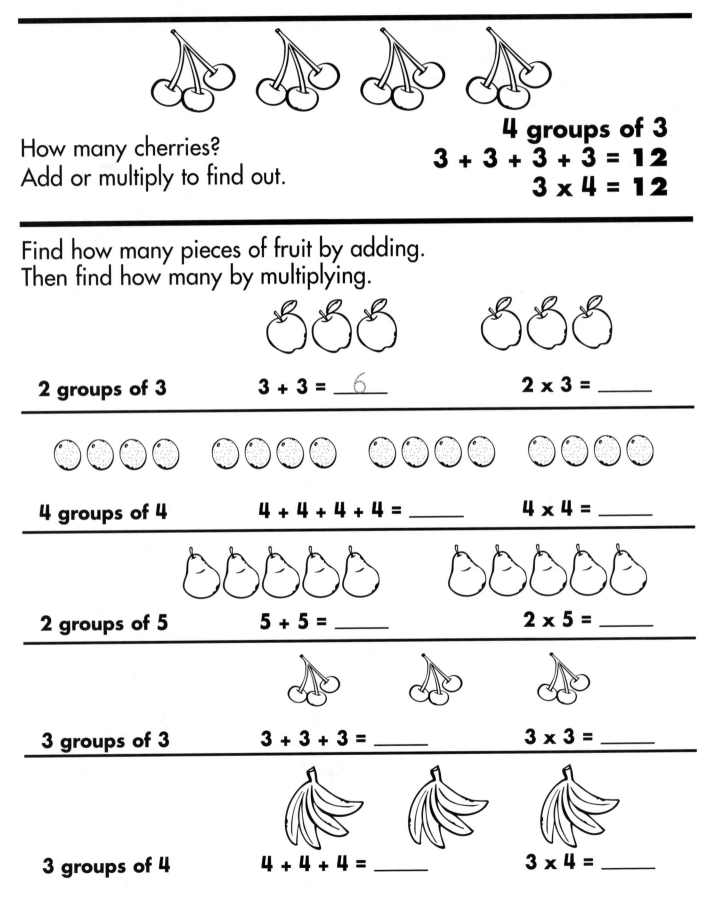

How many cherries?
Add or multiply to find out.

4 groups of 3
3 + 3 + 3 + 3 = 12
3 x 4 = 12

Find how many pieces of fruit by adding.
Then find how many by multiplying.

2 groups of 3   3 + 3 = ___6___   2 x 3 = _____

4 groups of 4   4 + 4 + 4 + 4 = _____   4 x 4 = _____

2 groups of 5   5 + 5 = _____   2 x 5 = _____

3 groups of 3   3 + 3 + 3 = _____   3 x 3 = _____

3 groups of 4   4 + 4 + 4 = _____   3 x 4 = _____

Relating repeated addition and multiplication

Special Delivery

Remember, with equal groups you can multiply.

On Monday, 3 bunnies got mail.
Each bunny got 2 letters.
How many letters in all?

$$\begin{array}{r} 2 \\ \times\ 3 \\ \hline 6 \end{array}$$

3 groups of 2   3 x 2 = 6

6 letters in all

Read each story problem. Multiply to find the answer.

1. **On Tuesday, 3 bunnies got mail.**
   Each bunny got 3 letters.
   How many letters in all? _____

2. **On Wednesday, 3 bunnies got mail.**
   Each bunny got 1 letter.
   How many letters in all? _____

3. **On Thursday, 2 bunnies got mail.**
   Each bunny got 2 letters.
   How many letters in all? _____

4. **On Friday, 2 bunnies got mail.**
   Each bunny got 3 letters.
   How many letters in all? _____

5. **On Saturday, 1 bunny got mail.**
   The bunny got 3 letters.
   How many letters in all? _____

Wrapping Up Numbers

Fill in the missing numbers.

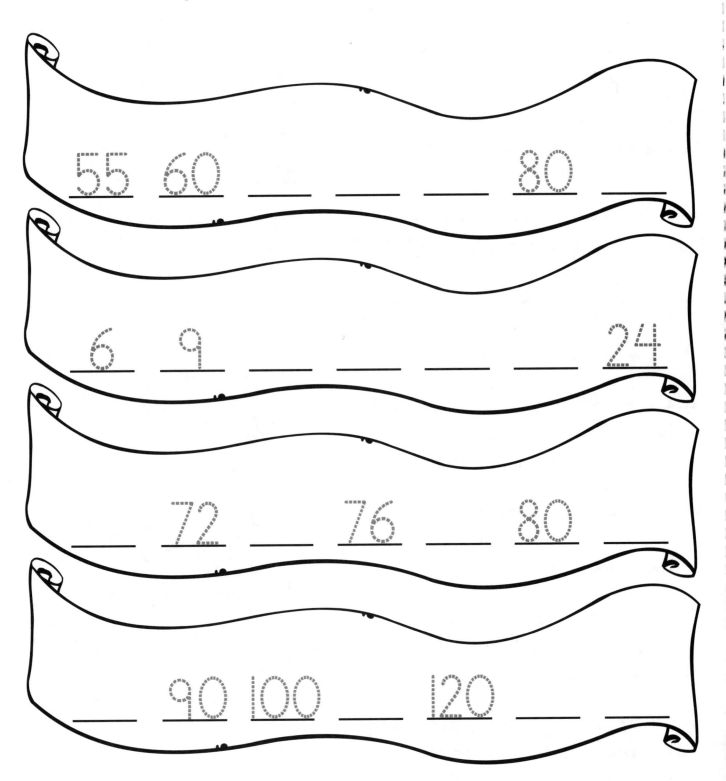

55 60 ___ ___ ___ 80 ___

6 9 ___ ___ ___ ___ 24

___ 72 ___ 76 ___ 80 ___

___ 90 100 ___ 120 ___

Counting by 2's, 3's, 5's, and 10's

Pattern Puzzles

Find the pattern. Write the missing numbers.

Getting Smaller

Write the numbers in order from **greatest** to **least**.

56	77	68	___ ___ ___
312	123	231	___ ___ ___
743	634	467	___ ___ ___
190	214	349	___ ___ ___
43	41	48	___ ___ ___
497	528	479	___ ___ ___
821	757	804	___ ___ ___
312	321	320	___ ___ ___
86	99	98	___ ___ ___
880	816	900	___ ___ ___
617	600	599	___ ___ ___
930	929	931	___ ___ ___
111	101	110	___ ___ ___

Ordering 2- and 3-digit numbers

Carnival of Numbers

Write the numbers for each clue.

Across

A. 4 hundreds 2 tens 6 ones
B. Eight hundred five
D. 200 + 70 + 8
F. Five hundred thirty-seven
G. 7 hundreds 2 tens 9 ones
I. Four hundred seventy-six
K. 800 + 10 + 2
L. Four hundred

Down

A. 400 + 90 + 2
C. 5 hundreds 1 ten 7 ones
E. Eight hundred sixty-nine
F. 500 + 70 + 4
H. 2 hundreds 3 tens 1 one
J. Seven hundred ninety

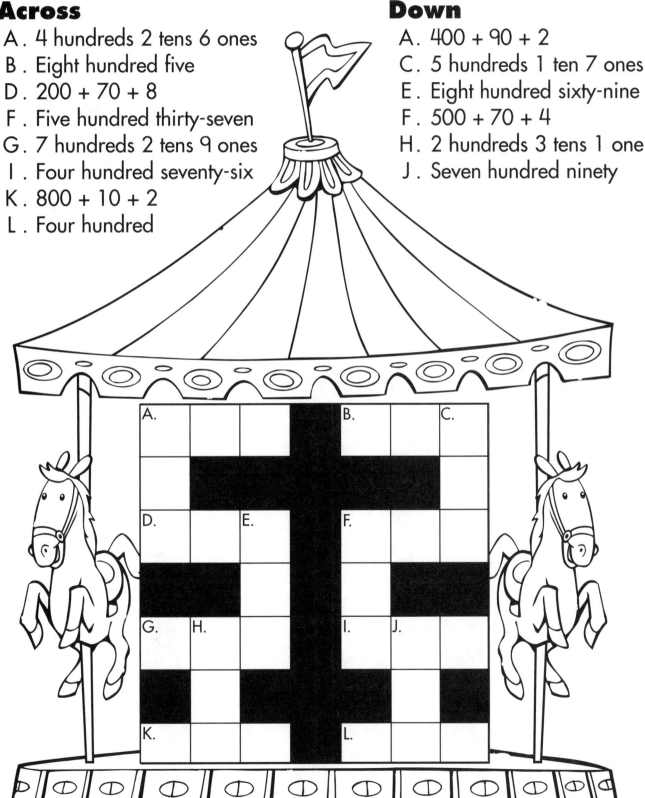

Reading and writing 3-digit numbers

45

Sign Sleuth

Fill in the missing signs.

5 ⊞ 3 = 8   4 □ 1 = 3   9 □ 4 = 5

7 □ 2 = 5   3 □ 3 = 6   3 □ 2 = 1

1 □ 6 = 7   4 □ 4 = 0   8 □ 6 = 2

12 □ 5 = 7   9 □ 2 = 11   18 □ 9 = 9

8 □ 6 = 14   13 □ 4 = 9   16 □ 8 = 8

8 □ 9 = 17   5 □ 3 = 2   8 □ 1 = 9

10 □ 5 = 5   15 □ 8 = 7   6 □ 6 = 12

14 □ 2 = 16   4 □ 8 = 12   11 □ 5 = 6

9 □ 3 = 12   17 □ 6 = 11   8 □ 2 = 10

Number Surprises

Rearrange each set of numbers to solve the math sentences.

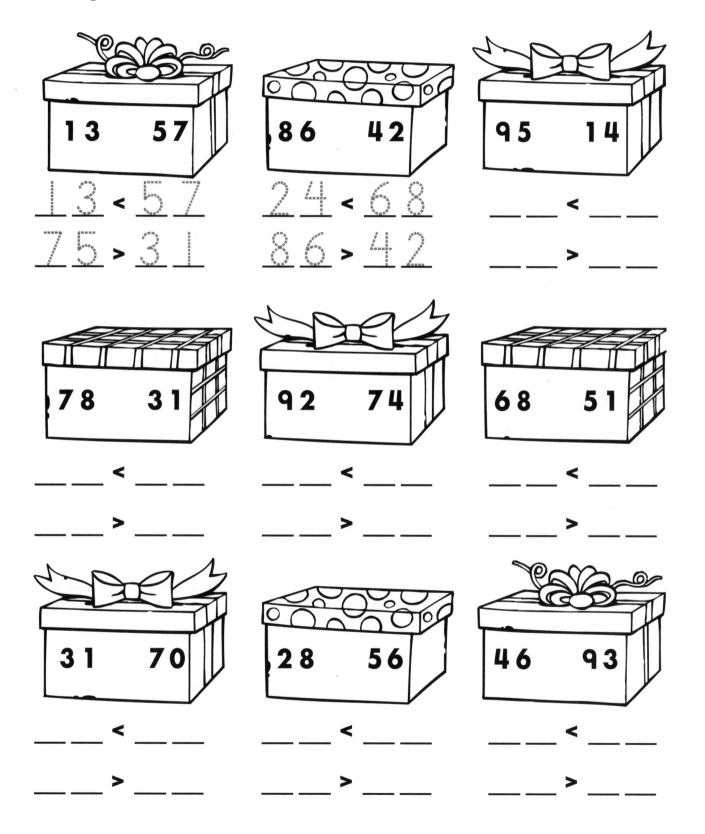

13   57

86   42

95   14

1 3 < 5 7
7 5 > 3 1

2 4 < 6 8
8 6 > 4 2

___ ___ < ___ ___
___ ___ > ___ ___

78   31

92   74

68   51

___ ___ < ___ ___
___ ___ > ___ ___

___ ___ < ___ ___
___ ___ > ___ ___

___ ___ < ___ ___
___ ___ > ___ ___

31   70

28   56

46   93

___ ___ < ___ ___
___ ___ > ___ ___

___ ___ < ___ ___
___ ___ > ___ ___

___ ___ < ___ ___
___ ___ > ___ ___

Using inequality signs to compare 2-digit numbers

47

Follow the Signs

Find the answer.

9 + 6	4 + 8	14 – 7	9 + 3	18 – 9
13 – 5	16 – 7	11 + 7	12 – 8	7 + 4
9 + 5	15 – 8	11 – 4	14 – 4	7 + 3
6 + 8	9 + 8	15 – 6	16 – 8	12 – 5
13 – 8	9 – 9	8 + 2	17 – 8	9 – 7

Practicing addition and subtraction facts to 18

Addition Trio

Add.

4	7	5	9	3
2	7	3	4	2
+ 9	+ 3	+ 5	+ 5	+ 8

6	7	3	6	1
7	8	2	6	5
+ 4	+ 3	+ 6	+ 5	+ 4

8	7	9	4	5
4	5	2	4	6
+ 4	+ 2	+ 4	+ 4	+ 2

3	6	2	9	8
7	8	8	3	1
+ 5	+ 1	+ 5	+ 3	+ 9

Adding three 1-digit numbers

49

Addition Review

Write the sum.

54	39	28	51	46
+ 36	+ 52	+ 44	+ 29	+ 25

63	50	84	7	16
+ 24	+ 75	+ 11	+ 89	+ 67

236	310	200	738	359
+ 143	+ 425	+ 354	+ 290	+ 427

563	704	353	624	168
+ 167	+ 298	+ 194	+ 319	+ 586

Read each story problem. Write a number sentence and solve.

At a garage sale, Arta's family sold 197 paperback books and 84 hardback books. How many books did they sell in all?

Mr. Green's class read 243 books in April and 328 books in May. How many books did they read in the two-month period?

_____

_____

Reviewing 2- and 3-digit addition with and without regrouping

Patterned Sums

Add. Circle the sums that are greater than 599.
What pattern do you see?

200	279	412	342	168
+ 400	+ 110	+ 213	+ 247	+ 321
(600)				

240	353	152	412	253
+ 410	+ 322	+ 345	+ 87	+ 243

509	400	620	321	230
+ 50	+ 300	+ 105	+ 123	+ 520

327	316	443	400	258
+ 261	+ 282	+ 332	+ 400	+ 341

622	313	500	674	600
+ 203	+ 130	+ 350	+ 201	+ 300

Adding 3-digit numbers without regrouping

Double-Digit Addition Trio

Add.

40	10	61	56	13
20	26	27	20	12
+30	+ 31	+ 10	+ 10	+ 11

20	23	30	14	10
22	61	12	43	22
+24	+ 15	+ 13	+20	+ 11

16	21	14	26	30
21	32	13	21	30
+50	+23	+22	+ 11	+30

18	20	20	41	52
10	34	16	27	12
+ 11	+ 14	+23	+20	+ 10

Adding three 2-digit numbers

Subtracting More Than Once

Subtract.

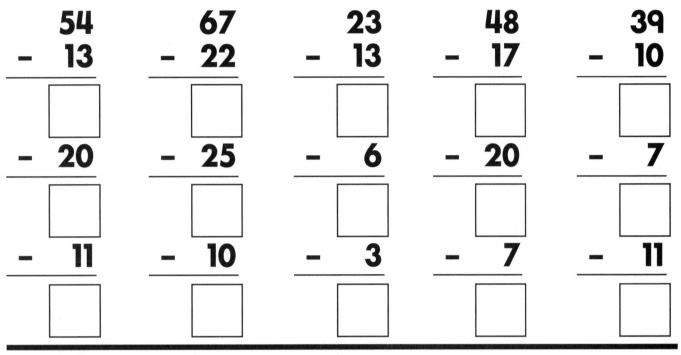

54	67	23	48	39
− 13	− 22	− 13	− 17	− 10
− 20	− 25	− 6	− 20	− 7
− 11	− 10	− 3	− 7	− 11

Subtract.

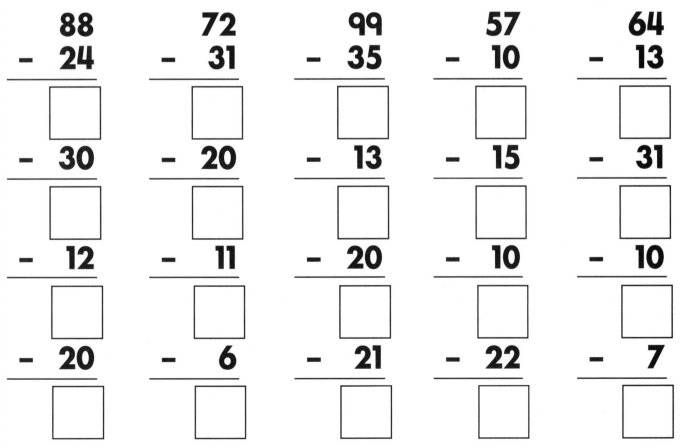

88	72	99	57	64
− 24	− 31	− 35	− 10	− 13
− 30	− 20	− 13	− 15	− 31
− 12	− 11	− 20	− 10	− 10
− 20	− 6	− 21	− 22	− 7

Subtraction Review

Subtract.

64 − 37	89 − 54	98 − 39	41 − 27	76 − 55
61 − 54	50 − 36	31 − 17	73 − 55	90 − 67
336 − 143	425 − 370	863 − 354	738 − 390	559 − 427
463 − 127	764 − 228	375 − 194	624 − 319	968 − 586

Read each story problem. Write a number sentence and solve.

Marci has 48 dolls and 75 stuffed animals. How many more stuffed animals than dolls does Marci have?

A total of 614 tickets are sold for a play. Of those, 341 are student tickets. How many tickets are not student tickets?

_____

_____

Reviewing 2- and 3-digit subtraction with and without regrouping

Domino Doubles

The domino has two sides.
Each side has 3 dots.
How many dots in all?

2 groups of 3 dots

2 x 3 = 6

6 dots in all

Multiply to find the total number of dots.

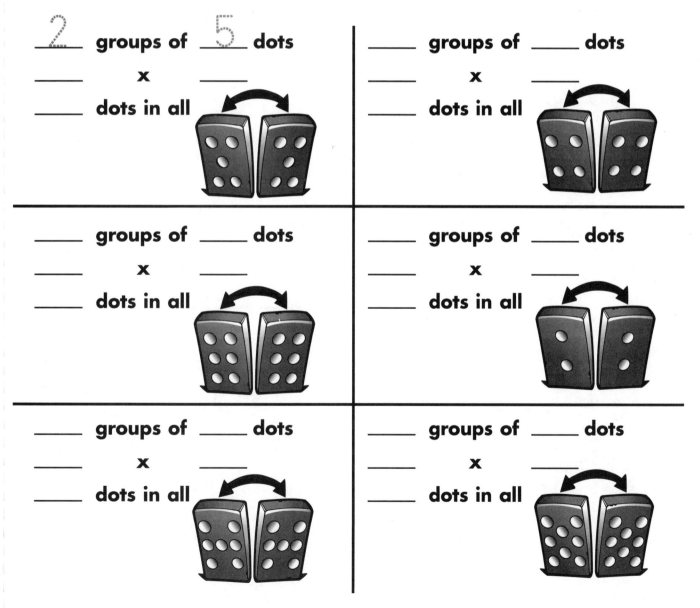

__2__ groups of __5__ dots

_____ x _____

_____ dots in all

_____ groups of _____ dots

_____ x _____

_____ dots in all

_____ groups of _____ dots

_____ x _____

_____ dots in all

_____ groups of _____ dots

_____ x _____

_____ dots in all

_____ groups of _____ dots

_____ x _____

_____ dots in all

_____ groups of _____ dots

_____ x _____

_____ dots in all

Measure It

Circle the correct answer.

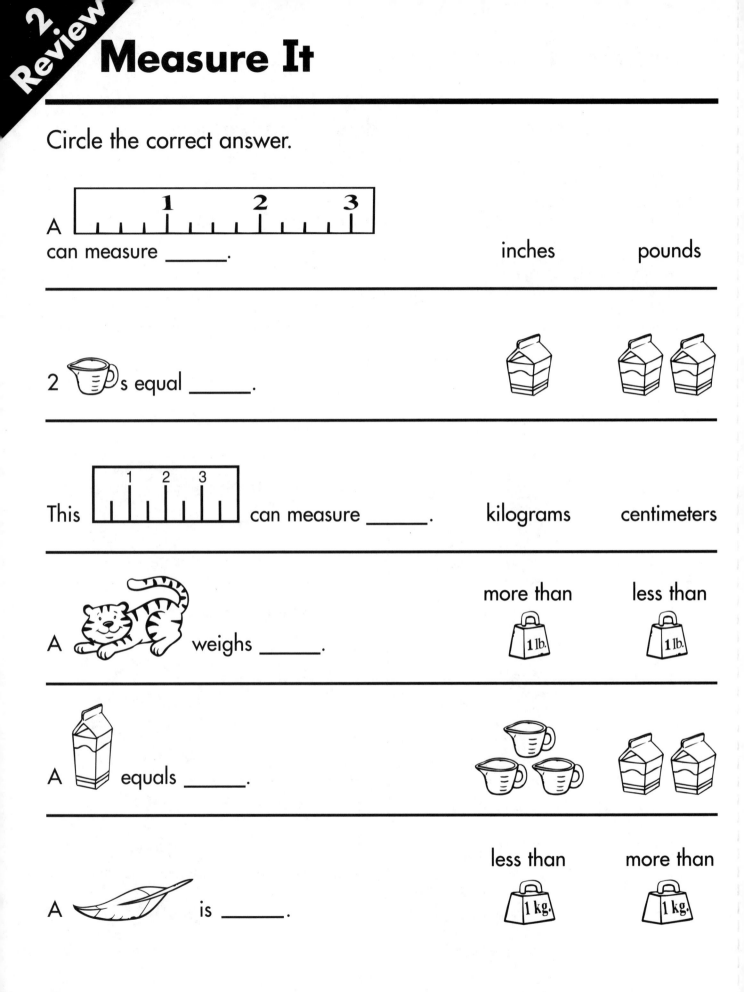

A [ruler 1 2 3]
can measure _____.   inches   pounds

2 [measuring cup]s equal _____.   [1 carton]   [2 cartons]

This [ruler 1 2 3] can measure _____.   kilograms   centimeters

A [tiger] weighs _____.   more than [1 lb.]   less than [1 lb.]

A [carton] equals _____.   [3 measuring cups]   [2 cartons]

A [feather] is _____.   less than [1 kg.]   more than [1 kg.]

Fraction Fun

Color one part. Circle the fraction that names the colored part.

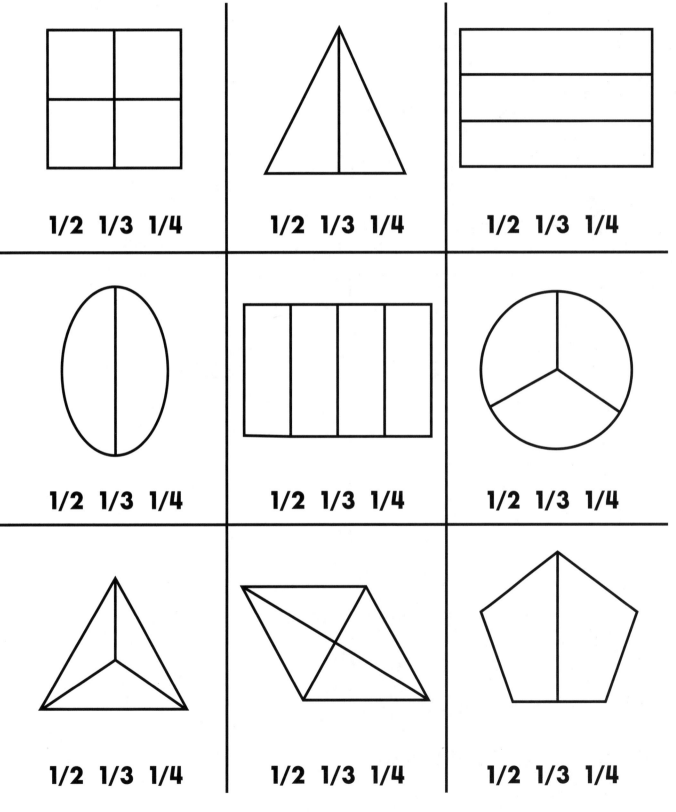

1/2 1/3 1/4   1/2 1/3 1/4   1/2 1/3 1/4

1/2 1/3 1/4   1/2 1/3 1/4   1/2 1/3 1/4

1/2 1/3 1/4   1/2 1/3 1/4   1/2 1/3 1/4

Pets, Anyone?

Each student was asked to name one pet.
Read the graph to answer the questions.

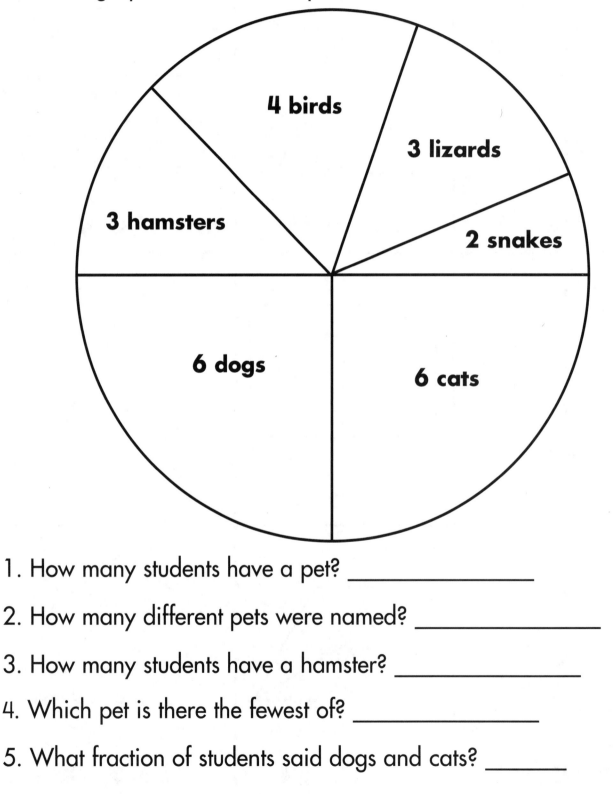

1. How many students have a pet? _____

2. How many different pets were named? _____

3. How many students have a hamster? _____

4. Which pet is there the fewest of? _____

5. What fraction of students said dogs and cats? _____

Interpreting a circle graph

What's the Temperature?

Circle the correct temperature.

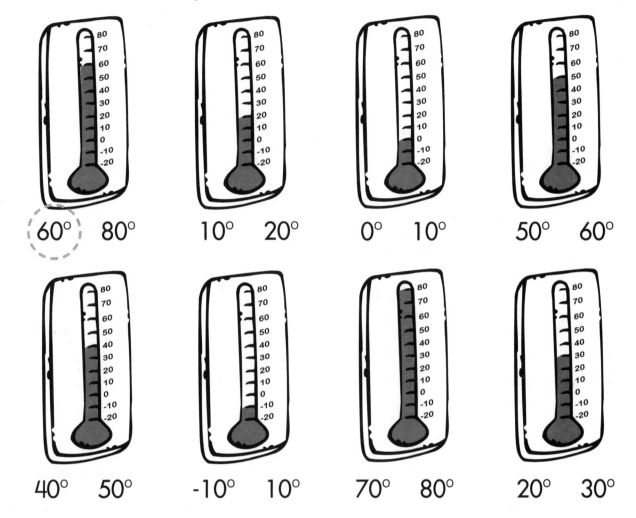

60° 80°   10° 20°   0° 10°   50° 60°

40° 50°   -10° 10°   70° 80°   20° 30°

Write the temperature.

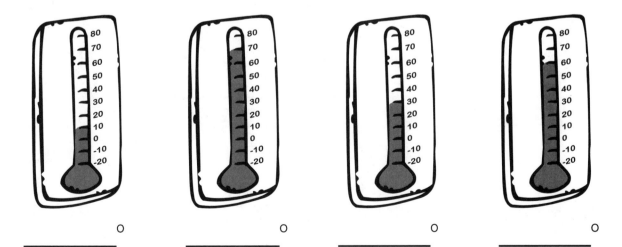

_____ °   _____ °   _____ °   _____ °

Money and Time Test

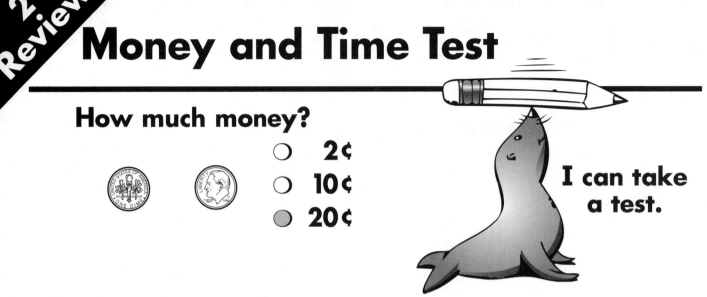

How much money?

- ○ 2¢
- ○ 10¢
- ● 20¢

I can take a test.

Fill in the circle next to the correct answer.

1. How much money?
- ○ 5¢
- ○ 23¢
- ○ 32¢

5. What time is it?
- ○ 8:15
- ○ 8:30
- ○ 3:30

2. How much money?
- ○ 10¢
- ○ 11¢
- ○ 21¢

6. What time is it?
- ○ 6:15
- ○ 6:30
- ○ 6:45

3. How much money?
- ○ 60¢
- ○ 50¢
- ○ 40¢

7. What time is it?
- ○ 2:00
- ○ 2:20
- ○ 4:10

4. How much money?
- ○ 29¢
- ○ 9¢
- ○ 14¢

8. What time is it?
- ○ 8:45
- ○ 8:55
- ○ 9:00

Testing money and time skills

Answer Key

Please take time to review the work your child has completed and remember to praise both success and effort. If your child makes a mistake, let him or her know that mistakes are a part of learning. Then explain the correct answer and how to find it. Taking the time to help your child and an active interest in his or her progress shows that you feel learning is important.

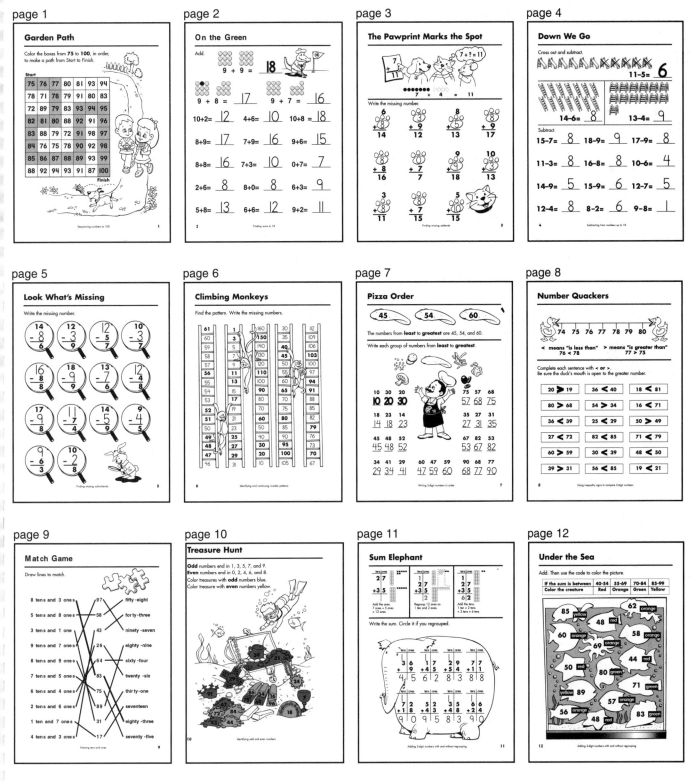

Hundreds, Tens, and Ones

Write how many hundreds, tens, and ones. Then write the number.

3 hundreds 5 tens 8 ones

2 hundreds 4 tens 3 ones — 243
3 hundreds 8 tens 7 ones — 187
5 hundreds 1 tens 6 ones — 516
4 hundreds 6 tens 1 ones — 461
3 hundreds 3 tens 3 ones — 333
3 hundreds 2 tens 9 ones — 329

Counting and writing groups of hundreds, tens, and ones   13

Diving for Treasure

hundreds	tens	ones
1	4	7
+ 5	3	2
		9

Add the ones.
7 ones + 2 ones = 9 ones

Add the tens.
4 tens + 3 tens = 7 tens

Add the hundreds.
1 hundred + 5 hundreds = 6 hundreds. The sum is 679.

First add the ones. Then add the tens. Then add the hundreds.

5 1 6 + 2 8 0 = 7 9 6
3 4 0 + 5 1 8 = 8 5 8
9 4 1 + 2 8 = 9 6 9
3 2 6 + 4 5 3 = 7 7 9
4 3 6 + 5 3 0 = 9 6 6
8 2 1 + 1 6 3 = 9 8 4
3 4 + 8 5 4 = 8 8 8
1 5 2 + 7 4 2 = 8 9 4
6 0 7 + 2 5 1 = 8 5 8

14   Adding 3-digit numbers without regrouping

Ready, Set, Regroup

hundreds	tens	ones
2	5	8
+ 3	9	4

Add the ones. There are 12 ones. Regroup 10 ones for 1 ten.

Add the tens. There are 15 tens. Regroup 10 tens for 1 hundred.

Add the hundreds. There are 6 hundreds. The sum is 652.

Add. Use the example above to help you.

4 3 2 + 2 8 3 = 7 1 5
2 4 8 + 3 4 6 = 5 9 4
2 5 6 + 3 3 3 = 5 8 9
3 6 5 + 3 7 9 = 7 4 4
1 2 5 + 4 9 = 1 7 4
7 8 4 + 1 6 5 = 9 4 9

Adding 3-digit numbers with and without regrouping   15

Sticker Math

Read each story problem. Write a number sentence and solve.

STICKER SHOP

1. One day, Mr. Perez sells 132 plain animal stickers and 257 puffy animal stickers. How many animal stickers does he sell that day?
132 + 257 = 389 stickers

2. Mr. Perez orders 527 new shiny stickers and 268 new puffy stickers. How many new stickers does Mr. Perez order?
527 + 268 = 795 stickers

3. Ms. Ross buys 87 race stickers and 125 happy face stickers. How many stickers does Ms. Ross buy?
125 + 87 = 212 stickers

4. Julie's scout troop buys 328 puffy stickers and 480 shiny stickers. How many stickers does the troop buy?
328 + 480 = 808 stickers

5. Mrs. Patel buys 249 "Good Work" stickers and 518 star stickers. How many stickers does Mrs. Patel buy?
249 + 518 = 767 stickers

6. The Sticker Club buys 375 animal stickers and 297 animal stickers. How many stickers does the club buy?
375 + 297 = 672 stickers

16   Solving addition story problems involving 2- and 3-digit numbers

Flying High

4 5 − 2 8 = 17
3 15 4 5 − 2 8 = 17
3 15 4 5 − 2 8 = 17

You cannot subtract 8 ones from 5 ones. Regroup 1 ten for 10 ones.

Subtract the ones. 15 ones − 8 ones = 7 ones

Subtract the tens. 3 tens − 2 tens = 1 ten. 45 − 28 = 17

Write the difference. Circle it if you regrouped.

2 6 − 9 = 17
6 8 − 45 = 23
7 2 − 54 = 18
4 7 − 8 = 39
3 2 − 18 = 14
3 2 − 27 = 5
9 8 − 48 = 50
6 0 − 24 = 36

Subtracting 2-digit numbers with and without regrouping   17

Winning Scores

Circle the greater score. Then subtract to find out by how many points the home team won.

HOME 53 VISITOR 42 → 11
HOME 63 VISITOR 51 → 12
HOME 54 VISITOR 10 → 10
HOME 75 VISITOR 61 → 14
HOME 70 VISITOR 53 → 17
HOME 71 VISITOR 55 → 16
HOME 84 VISITOR 49 → 35
HOME 60 VISITOR 42 → 18
HOME 90 VISITOR 81 → 9
HOME 94 VISITOR 76 → 18
HOME 83 VISITOR 67 → 16
HOME 78 VISITOR 70 → 8

18   Subtracting 3-digit numbers with and without regrouping

Dive Into Subtraction

hundreds	tens	ones
8	4	9
− 5	1	2
		7

Subtract the ones. 9 ones − 2 ones = 7 ones

Subtract the tens. 4 tens − 1 ten = 3 tens

Subtract the hundreds. 8 hundreds − 5 hundreds = 3 hundreds. The difference is 337.

Subtract.

9 7 6 − 3 5 3 = 6 2 3
7 8 5 − 4 8 1 = 3 0 4
5 8 6 − 2 5 4 = 3 3 2
8 3 6 − 5 2 0 = 3 1 6
4 9 8 − 2 5 1 = 2 4 7
3 9 2 − 2 = 3 0 0

Subtracting 3-digit numbers without regrouping   19

All Aboard

hundreds	tens	ones
7	3	9
− 4	5	3

Subtract the ones. 9 ones − 3 ones = 6 ones

You cannot subtract 5 tens from 3 tens. Regroup 1 hundred for 10 tens.

Subtract the hundreds. 6 hundreds − 4 hundreds = 2 hundreds. The difference is 286.

Subtract. Regroup if you need to.

4 3 − 1 8 7 = ...
4 2 − 3 4 6 = 4 0 6
6 4 6 − 5 3 3 = 1 1 3
7 6 − 3 7 1 = 4 9 4
7 4 − 1 6 5 = 1 5 0
7 4 − 1 6 5 = 5 1 9

20   Subtracting 3-digit numbers with and without regrouping

Take Me Out to the Ball Game

Read each story problem. Write a number sentence and solve.

1. There are 387 boys and 410 girls at the Stars game. How many more girls than boys are at the game?
410 − 387 = 23 more girls

2. There are 797 children and 912 adults at the Stars game. How many more adults than children are at the game?
912 − 797 = 115 more adults

3. Manny sells 425 sodas and 670 bottled waters. How many more bottled waters than sodas are sold?
670 − 425 = 245 more bottled waters

4. Jane sells 459 bags of peanuts and 953 hot dogs. How many more hot dogs than peanuts are sold?
953 − 459 = 494 more hot dogs

5. The Stars sell 564 pennants. Of those, 181 are small pennants and the rest are large pennants. How many large pennants are sold?
564 − 181 = 383 large pennants

6. The Stars give away 175 t-shirts. All but 38 of them are given to children. How many t-shirts are given to children?
175 − 38 = 137 t-shirts

7. Mr. Patel has 800 Stars baseball caps to sell. He sells all but 282 of them. How many caps does Mr. Patel sell?
800 − 282 = 518 caps

8. The Stars play 65 games at home out of a total of 123 games. How many games are played away from home?
123 − 65 = 58 games

Solving subtraction story problems involving 2- and 3-digit numbers   21

At the Zoo

Use an inch ruler to measure each path on the map. Write about how many inches.

How long is the path:

1. From the entrance to the monkey? — 2 inches
2. From the entrance to the snake? — 5 inches
3. From the monkey to the bird? — 1 inches
4. From the snack bar to the seal? — 1 inches
5. From the elephant to the lion? — 1 inches
6. From the lion to the snake? — 3 inches

22   Measuring paths in inches

Find Sam's Sneaker

Use a centimeter ruler to measure the length of each sneaker. Sam's sneaker is 9 centimeters long. Find and color Sam's sneaker.

5 centimeters
10 centimeters
9 centimeters
13 centimeters
10 centimeters

Measuring length in centimeters   23

How Much Does It Hold?

less than 1 liter   1 liter   more than 1 liter

Color the things that hold more than 1 liter red.
Color the things that hold less than 1 liter yellow.

yellow   yellow   red
yellow   red   red
red

24   Comparing the capacity of containers with 1 liter

Cups, Pints, and Quarts

1 cup   2 cups = 1 pint   4 cups = 1 quart

Color the cups to show the same amounts.

Comparing the capacity of cups, pints, and quarts   25

Weighing Pounds

This spaghetti weighs 1 pound. Another way to write pound is lb.

Color the things that weigh more than 1 pound red.
Color the things that weigh less than 1 pound blue.

red   red   blue
blue   red   red
blue   blue   red

26   Comparing weights to 1 pound

Kilograms

Another way to write kilogram is kg.

less than 1 kilogram   about 1 kilogram   more than 1 kilogram

Color the things that are more than 1 kilogram green.
Color the things that are less than 1 kilogram orange.

green   green   orange
orange   green   green
green   orange   green

Comparing weights to 1 kilogram   27

Food for Sharing

Color 1/2 red.

Color 1/3 green.

Color 1/4 orange.

28   Recognizing halves, thirds, and fourths

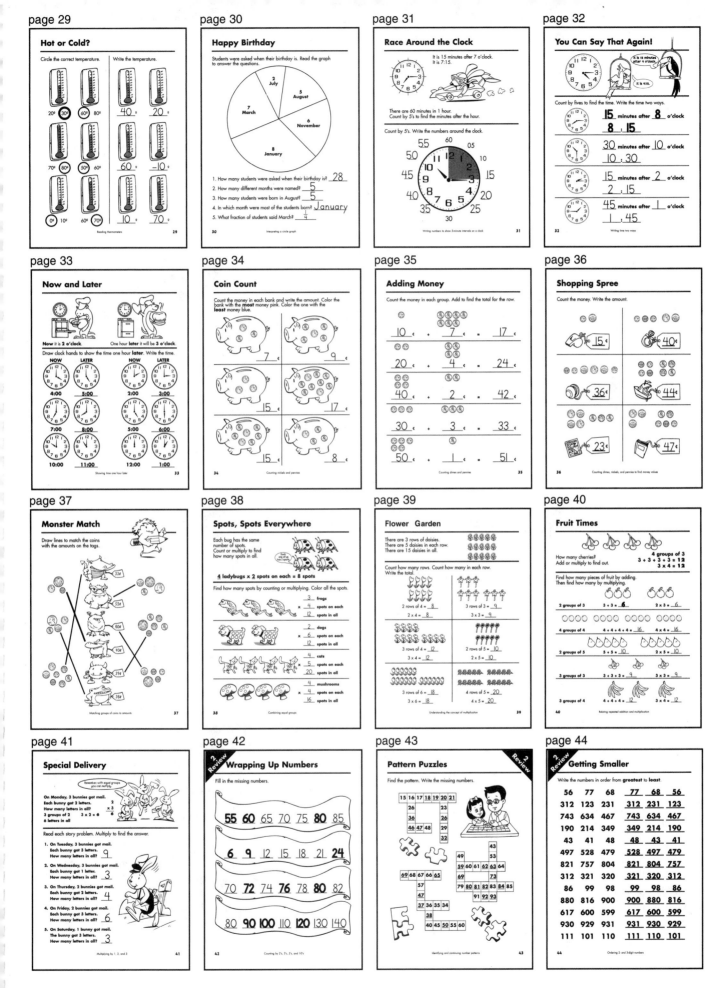

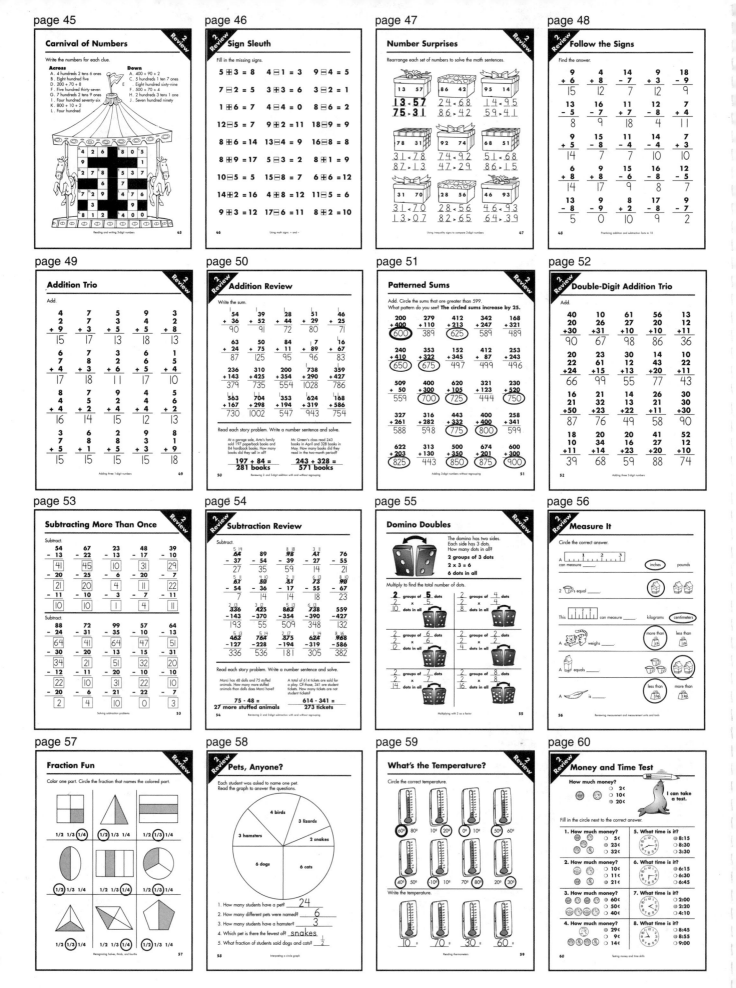

page 45

Carnival of Numbers

Write the numbers for each clue.

Across
A. 4 hundreds 2 tens 6 ones
B. Eight hundred five
D. 200 + 70 + 8
F. Five hundred thirty-seven
G. 7 hundreds 2 tens 9 ones
I. Four hundred seventy-six
K. 800 + 10 + 2
L. Four hundred

Down
A. 400 + 90 + 2
C. 5 hundreds 1 ten 7 ones
E. Eight hundred sixty-nine
F. 500 + 70 + 4
H. 2 hundreds 3 tens 1 one
J. Seven hundred ninety

Reading and writing 3-digit numbers   45

page 46

Sign Sleuth

Fill in the missing signs.

5 ⊞ 3 = 8   4 ⊟ 1 = 3   9 ⊟ 4 = 5

7 ⊟ 2 = 5   3 ⊞ 3 = 6   3 ⊟ 2 = 1

1 ⊞ 6 = 7   4 ⊟ 4 = 0   8 ⊟ 6 = 2

12 ⊟ 5 = 7   9 ⊞ 2 = 11   18 ⊟ 9 = 9

8 ⊞ 6 = 14   13 ⊟ 4 = 9   16 ⊟ 8 = 8

8 ⊞ 9 = 17   5 ⊟ 3 = 2   8 ⊞ 1 = 9

10 ⊟ 5 = 5   15 ⊟ 8 = 7   6 ⊞ 6 = 12

14 ⊟ 2 = 16   4 ⊞ 8 = 12   11 ⊟ 5 = 6

9 ⊞ 3 = 12   17 ⊟ 6 = 11   8 ⊞ 2 = 10

46   Using math signs: + and −

page 47

Number Surprises

Rearrange each set of numbers to solve the math sentences.

13 > 57 → **13 < 57**
75 > 31 → **75 > 31**

24 < 68 → **86 > 42**

14 < 95 → **14 < 95**
59 < 41 → **59 > 41**

78 < 78 → **31 < 78**
87 > 13 → **87 > 13**

92 74 → **74 > 29**
47 > 29

68 51 → **51 < 68**
86 > 15

31 70 → **31 < 70**
13 < 07

28 56 → **28 < 56**
82 > 65

46 93 → **46 < 93**
64 > 39

Using inequality signs to compare 2-digit numbers   47

page 48

Follow the Signs

Find the answer.

9 + 6 15	4 + 8 12	14 − 7 7	9 + 3 12	18 − 9 9
13 − 5 8	16 − 7 9	11 + 7 18	12 − 8 4	7 + 4 11
9 + 5 14	15 − 8 7	11 − 4 7	14 − 4 10	7 + 3 10
6 + 8 14	9 + 8 17	15 − 6 9	16 − 8 8	12 − 5 7
13 − 8 5	9 − 9 0	8 + 2 10	17 − 8 9	9 − 7 2

48   Practicing addition and subtraction facts to 18

page 49

Addition Trio

Add.

4 2 + 9 15	7 7 + 3 17	5 4 + 5 13	9 4 + 5 18	3 2 + 8 13
6 7 + 4 17	7 8 + 3 18	3 2 + 6 11	6 6 + 5 17	1 5 + 4 10
8 4 + 4 16	7 5 + 2 14	9 2 + 4 15	4 6 + 2 12	6 5 + 2 13
3 7 + 5 15	6 8 + 1 15	2 8 + 5 15	9 3 + 3 15	8 1 + 9 18

Adding three 1-digit numbers   49

page 50

Addition Review

Write the sum.

54 + 36 90	39 + 52 91	28 + 44 72	51 + 29 80	46 + 25 71
63 + 24 87	50 + 75 125	84 + 11 95	7 + 89 96	16 + 67 83
236 + 143 379	310 + 425 735	200 + 354 554	738 + 290 1028	359 + 427 786
563 + 167 730	704 + 298 1002	353 + 194 547	624 + 319 943	168 + 586 754

Read each story problem. Write a number sentence and solve.

At a garage sale, Arto's family sold 197 paperback books and 84 hardback books. How many books did they sell in all?

197 + 84 = 281 books

Mr. Green's class read 243 books in April and 328 books in May. How many books did they read in the two-month period?

243 + 328 = 571 books

50   Reviewing 2- and 3-digit addition with and without regrouping

page 51

Patterned Sums

Add. Circle the sums that are greater than 599.
What pattern do you see? **The circled sums increase by 25.**

200 +400 (600)	279 +110 389	412 +213 (625)	342 +247 589	168 +321 489
240 +410 (650)	353 +322 (675)	152 +345 497	412 + 87 499	253 +243 496
509 + 50 559	400 +300 (700)	620 +105 (725)	321 +123 444	230 +520 (750)
327 +261 588	316 +282 598	443 +332 (775)	400 +400 (800)	258 +341 599
622 +203 (825)	313 +130 443	500 +350 (850)	674 +201 (875)	600 +300 (900)

Adding 3-digit numbers without regrouping   51

page 52

Double-Digit Addition Trio

Add.

40 20 +30 90	10 26 +31 67	61 27 +10 98	56 20 +10 86	13 12 +11 36
20 22 +24 66	23 61 +15 99	30 12 +13 55	14 43 +20 77	10 22 +11 43
16 21 +50 87	32 23 +21 76	14 13 +22 49	26 21 +11 58	30 30 +30 90
18 10 +11 39	20 34 +14 68	20 16 +23 59	41 27 +20 88	52 12 +10 74

52   Adding three 2-digit numbers

page 53

Subtracting More Than Once

Subtract.

| 54
− 13
41
− 20
21
− 11
10 | 67
− 22
45
− 25
20
− 10
10 | 23
− 13
10
− 6
4 | 48
− 17
31
− 20
11
− 7
4 | 39
− 10
29
− 7
22
− 11
11 |

Subtract.

| 88
− 24
64
− 30
34
− 12
22
− 20
2 | 72
− 31
41
− 20
21
− 11
10
− 6
4 | 99
− 35
64
− 13
51
− 31
20
− 21 | 57
− 10
47
− 15
32
− 10
22
− 22 | 64
− 13
51
− 31
20
− 10
10
− 7
3 |

Solving subtraction problems   53

page 54

Subtraction Review

Subtract.

64 − 37 27	89 − 54 35	98 − 39 59	41 − 27 14	76 − 55 21
61 − 54 7	50 − 36 14	31 − 17 14	73 − 55 18	90 − 67 23
336 − 143 193	862 − 370 55	863 − 354 509	738 − 390 348	559 − 427 132
463 − 127 336	764 − 228 536	375 − 194 181	624 − 319 305	968 − 586 382

Read each story problem. Write a number sentence and solve.

Marci has 48 dolls and 75 stuffed animals. How many more stuffed animals than dolls does Marci have?

75 − 48 = 27 more stuffed animals

A total of 614 tickets are sold for a play. Of those, 341 are student tickets. How many tickets are not student tickets?

614 − 341 = 273 tickets

54   Reviewing 2- and 3-digit subtraction with and without regrouping

page 55

Domino Doubles

The domino has two sides. Each side has 3 dots. How many dots in all?

2 groups of 3 dots
2 × 3 = 6
6 dots in all

Multiply to find the total number of dots.

2 groups of 5 dots
2 × 5
10 dots in all

2 groups of 4 dots
2 × 4
8 dots in all

2 groups of 6 dots
2 × 6
12 dots in all

2 groups of 2 dots
2 × 2
4 dots in all

2 groups of 7 dots
2 × 7
14 dots in all

2 groups of 8 dots
2 × 8
16 dots in all

Multiplying with 2 as a factor   55

page 56

Measure It

Circle the correct answer.

A can measure (inches)   pounds

2 ___'s equal

This ___ can measure   kilograms   (centimeters)

A ___ weighs   (more than)   less than

A ___ equals

A ___ is   less than   (more than)

56   Reviewing measurement and measurement units and tools

page 57

Fraction Fun

Color one part. Circle the fraction that names the colored part.

1/2 1/3 (1/4)
(1/2) 1/3 1/4
(1/2) 1/3 1/4

(1/2) 1/3 1/4
1/2 1/3 (1/4)
(1/2) 1/3 1/4

1/2 (1/3) 1/4
1/2 1/3 (1/4)
(1/2) 1/3 1/4

Recognizing halves, thirds, and fourths   57

page 58

Pets, Anyone?

Each student was asked to name one pet. Read the graph to answer the questions.

4 birds
3 lizards
3 hamsters
2 snakes
6 dogs
6 cats

1. How many students have a pet?   **24**
2. How many different pets were named?   **6**
3. How many students have a hamster?   **3**
4. Which pet is there the fewest of?   **snakes**
5. What fraction of students said dogs and cats?   **1/2**

58   Interpreting a circle graph

page 59

What's the Temperature?

Circle the correct temperature.

(60°) 80°   10° 20°   0° 10°   50° (60°)

(40°) 50°   10° 10°   70° (80°)   20° 30°

Write the temperature.

10°   **70°**   **30°**   **60°**

Reading thermometers   59

page 60

Money and Time Test

How much money?
○ 2¢
○ 10¢
● 20¢

I can take a test.

Fill in the circle next to the correct answer.

1. How much money?
○ 5¢
● 23¢
○ 32¢

2. How much money?
● 10¢
○ 11¢
○ 21¢

3. How much money?
○ 60¢
● 50¢
○ 40¢

4. How much money?
○ 29¢
● 9¢
○ 14¢

5. What time is it?
● 8:15
○ 8:30
○ 3:30

6. What time is it?
○ 6:15
● 6:30
○ 6:45

7. What time is it?
○ 2:00
● 2:20
○ 4:10

8. What time is it?
● 8:45
○ 8:55
○ 9:00

60   Testing money and time skills